INTRODUCING

Learning and Memory

MEMORY
IS MAPPED BY
DIFFERENT PLACES
THAT I CAN VISIT
IN A SWIFT MENTAL
JOURNEY...

Ziauddin Sardar, Richard Appignanesi and Ralph Edney

D0094710

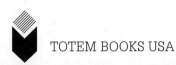

ICON BOOKS UK   TOTEM BOOKS USA

Published in the UK in 2002
by Icon Books Ltd., Grange Road,
Duxford, Cambridge CB2 4QF
E-mail: info@iconbooks.co.uk
www.iconbooks.co.uk

Sold in the UK, Europe, South Africa
and Asia by Faber and Faber Ltd.,
3 Queen Square, London WC1N 3AU
or their agents

Distributed in the UK, Europe,
South Africa and Asia by
Macmillan Distribution Ltd.,
Houndmills, Basingstoke RG21 6XS

Published in Australia in 2002
by Allen & Unwin Pty. Ltd.,
PO Box 8500, 83 Alexander Street,
Crows Nest, NSW 2065

Published in the USA in 2002
by Totem Books
Inquiries to: Icon Books Ltd.,
Grange Road, Duxford,
Cambridge CB2 4QF, UK

Distributed to the trade in the USA by
National Book Network Inc.,
4720 Boston Way, Lanham,
Maryland 20706

Distributed in Canada by
Penguin Books Canada,
10 Alcorn Avenue, Suite 300,
Toronto, Ontario M4V 3B2

ISBN 1 84046 350 3

Printed and bound in the UK
by Biddles Ltd., Guildford and King's Lynn

Talking pictures ...

Alice was beginning to get very tired of sitting by her sister on the bank and of having nothing to do. Once or twice she had peeped into the book her sister was reading, but it had no pictures or conversations in it.

Pages reproduced from other books in the *Introducing* series will be indicated like this:

watch out for this tab ...

Graphic aids to learning

How right Lewis Carroll was. But it's not just children who think of the world in terms of graphic images. In his other life, Lewis Carroll, or rather **Charles Lutwidge Dodgson** (1832–98) of Oxford University, was a logician and mathematician. His "Alice" books and poems are built on mathematical (il)logic and paradoxes.

Pictures come before words

One of the greatest thinkers, **Albert Einstein** (1879–1955), conducted his famous "thought experiments" in terms of pictures. He confessed: "My particular ability does not lie in mathematical calculation, but rather in visualizing effects, possibilities and consequences." Einstein dreamed $E = mc^2$. He *saw* it in his mind before knowing what it was.

INTRODUCING

Einstein

I PICTURED MYSELF RIDING ON A BEAM OF LIGHT, HOLDING A CLOCK, WHEN WORKING ON THE THEORY OF RELATIVITY

Impossible according to the principle of relativity.

Damn! There goes my image again. I keep telling them not to go 186,000 miles-per-second when I'm shaving.

The concord of words and pictures

The greatest logician of the 20th century, **Ludwig Wittgenstein** (1889–1951), understood language as a *picture* of the world. "A picture can depict any reality whose form it has … ." Language can picture the world because they both share the *logical form* of reality. Of course, it's not so simple as that. There are quicksands of ambiguity in the "language game".

POINTING

In this picture of the way we learn language, it is **pointing** and the words "this" and "that" that make the connection between word and meaning.

Pointing would then be the fundamental form of explanation linking words to the world.

HOW DOES AN ILLUSTRATOR **PICTURE** THE AMBIGUITIES THAT WITTGENSTEIN IS TRYING TO UNTANGLE?

THIS CHAIR

Judy Groves: illustrator

6

Lewis Carroll had already foreseen the language "booby traps" that preoccupied Wittgenstein. Let's go back to Alice …

Which makes the point – is the text solely in control of meaning, or does illustration essentially add to it? Let's dig into this …

A storyboard example

Introducing books crucially depend on the composition of a *storyboard*. This is the "synapse" which links the nerve-ends of text to image. It is created by an editorial process that transforms the text into a *script* responsive to illustration. Here is a sample page of *Introducing Critical Theory*, as originally produced by the author …

Barthes also argued against the cult of the author, going so far as to proclaim the 'death of the author' in the traditional sense – by which he meant the grand, heroic 'Author' passing on his words of wisdom to a grateful, and essentially passive, public. The author was viewed instead by Barthes as a channel through which language 'spoke', and readers were argued to be at least as much creators of narratives as authors were: 'the birth of the reader must be at the cost of the death of the Author'.

The text is not only edited for information requirements. It undergoes a "change of behaviour" from non-fiction message to *visual signification*. This is a process of scripting familiar in comic-book storyboarding, but employed here on documentary fact …

The text looks like this after storyboard editing …

The Death of the Author

Barthes also argued against the cult of the author, *In a notorious essay of 1968,* ~~going so far as to~~ proclaim the "death of the author" ~~in the traditional sense — by which~~ He meant the ~~grand~~ *traditional* heroic "Author" passing on his words of wisdom to a grateful and essentially passive, public. *I view* The author ~~was viewed~~ instead ~~by Barthes~~ as a channel through which language "spoke" *leaks* and Readers ~~were argued to be~~ *are* at least as much creators of narratives as authors ~~are~~ *are* ~~were~~ "The birth of the reader must be at the cost of the death of the Author."

Richard Appignanesi: editor

Let's see how this page will appear in final graphic resolution …

The Death of the Author

Barthes also argued against the cult of the author.

In a notorious essay of 1968, he even proclaimed the "death of the author". He meant the traditional, heroic "Author" passing on his words of wisdom to a grateful, and essentially passive, public.

I view the author instead as a channel through which language "speaks" ...

Readers are at least as much creators of narratives as authors are. "The birth of the reader must be at the cost of the death of the Author."

Combining the assets

Illustration achieves what its Latin root says: *lustrare* – it "lights up" the text. Where does the reader look first? At the light – at the pictures. But that's not entirely true. *Introducing* books really combine two texts: a written text and a visual text. The mind is engaged by reading text and image in *continuity*.

Oscar Zarate: illustrator

So, let's begin with the question – what is "learning"?

What is learning?

Learning is not just one of the most important features of a civil society. It is *the* foundation of civilization. Through learning …

- We become aware of ourselves and the world around us.

- We acquire a framework to understand and define problems that surround us.

- We develop tools, techniques and other problem-solving methods that support us.

- We acquire understanding and knowledge, and hence generate progress.

As the British science-fiction writer and social reformer **H. G. Wells** (1866–1946) remarked …

HUMAN HISTORY IS MORE AND MORE A RACE BETWEEN LEARNING AND CATASTROPHE

But what exactly is learning? There are different kinds of learning.
Learning to use a knife and fork or to tie one's shoe is not the same
as learning to overcome a phobia, such as fear of the dark.

How do we reconcile these different forms of learning? Is there something
inherent in human nature that enables us to learn? Or indeed, are we born
with forms of innate knowledge?

Innate or acquired knowledge?

For centuries, metaphysicians believed that we have knowledge of the world apart from our senses.

The metaphysicians pointed to mathematics and geometry as proof of their case. Such discoveries were made in ancient civilizations just by thinking, not by observing.

Then, during the Renaissance, the West discovered that mathematical discoveries are not about knowledge of objects, but the arrangement of symbols. Mathematical knowledge has to be tested "out there", in the "real world" – and that is not possible without observation.

When German mathematician **Karl Gauss** (1777–1855) realized that there is more than one geometry, and that other (non-Euclidean) geometries can be invented, metaphysicians were dealt a serious blow.

MATHEMATICS, IT TURNS OUT, PROVIDES US WITH USEFUL STEPS IN ARGUMENTS, BUT CANNOT REALLY GIVE US NEW FACTS ABOUT THE WORLD

KNOWLEDGE STARTS FROM EXPERIENCE

The enigma of perception

Still, some animals do seem to have innate knowledge. Migrating birds, for example, "know" where to go, even though we don't know how they know. But what happens when an animal or a person is brought up in darkness and then exposed to light? What do they perceive? Can we see how perception develops?

But then they can become depressed at flaking paint on a wall, at the drabness of the world, can begin to dislike sunrise and sunset, and, as studies show, some even contemplate suicide!

One of the main problems of learning to see is perception of depth – people with recovered eyesight have great difficulty in adjusting to depth.

In the late 1950s, American child psychologist Eleanor Gibson designed an experiment to see whether a baby would crawl over a ledge. The ledge was constructed with a thick glass over the drop. Babies would come to no harm if they crawled over the edge. The babies, however, did not do that. From crawling age, they had an understanding of a "drop" and did not go there.

Learning to see

Can we, from the Gibson experiment, conclude that babies have some innate notion of perception? Or do we learn perception from experience? How, in fact, do we learn to see?

The Alexandrian mathematician **Euclid** (323–285 BC) speculated on vision in his *Optics*.

The Arab physicist ibn al-Haytham, known in the West as **Alhazen** (c. 965–1038), realized that Euclid's concept of the eye was wrong.

*He went on to invent the first **camera obscura**, a pin-hole camera – but did not tell us that the images were inverted.*

Is the eye a camera?

Daniele Barbaro (1513–70), Venetian geometer and author of *Practica della Perspectiva* (1568–9), one of the most respected books on linear perspective during the Renaissance, replaced the hole with a lens.

What do artists see?

How did the Dutch painter **Jan Vermeer** (1632–75) achieve his magical realism? It is believed that he employed a *camera obscura* and lenses as optical aids to obtain his miraculous reflections of light on pearls, silks and wine-glasses.

Artists do not "paint what they see" – a self-contradictory notion, in any case. It would be more accurate to say that artists represent the *conventions of seeing* accepted by different societies. The renowned art historian E.H. Gombrich writes in *Art and Illusion* (1960): "What we call seeing is invariably coloured and shaped by our knowledge (or belief) of what we see."

WE CAN NEVER NEATLY SEPARATE WHAT WE SEE FROM WHAT WE KNOW OR REMEMBER

So the eye is not a camera. Nor does the eye produce pictures in the brain. What the eyes do is to give the brain information in the form of pulses of electricity. The patterns that these pulses give represent objects. For example, the words on this page have meaning for you because you know the language in which they are written.

Deceiving the eye

A line drawing can represent more than one thing.

Ambiguous figures illustrate how the brain can be misled. This figure, for example, alternates spontaneously. Sometimes it is seen as two opposing faces, sometimes as a white urn surrounded by a black area. To view the figure, we need to make a perceptual decision: how are we going to see it? What is "noise" and what is the "signal"?

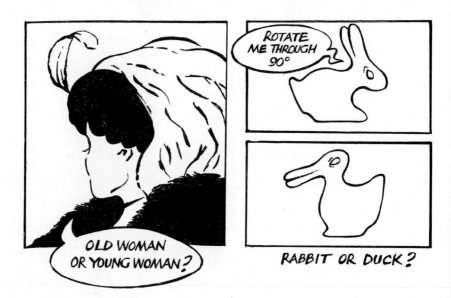

The Ames room

Here we are presented with a distorted room. The wall and windows are arranged to suggest a normal room, but the further wall in fact recedes from the observer. The figure on the left is in fact further away.

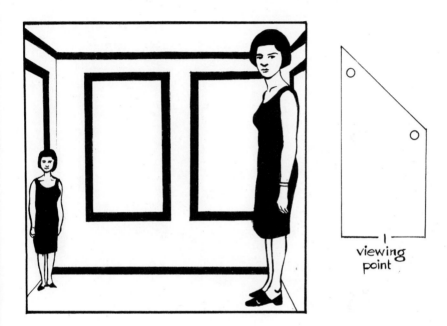

To make sense of the situation, and solve this visual puzzle, we look for clues to see how we are being deceived.

Perception is therefore based upon evidence. When we view something, we make the "best bet" as to what we are seeing. So perception turns out to be a problem-solving activity.

Our ability to perceive obviously plays an important part in learning. But the concept of learning is also deeply connected to another ability – our ability to *remember*. Indeed, learning is inconceivable without memory.

Defining memory

Memory is the ability of the mind to store and recall previous thoughts and experiences. Very little of human experience – from our self-awareness to the ability to reason – would be possible without our ability to remember.

Opinion is divided on the mechanisms of memory. Some believe that there is a single store of data into which everything is placed. But most believe that there are different systems – a **short-term memory** which retains information only for a few seconds, and a **long-term memory** which retains information for many years.

Various methods have been devised to improve long-term memory, the best-known being *mnemonics*, or rules for encoding new information into an easily remembered form.

Mnemonic systems

Mnemonics is defined as the art of improving the memory, or a system to aid the memory. Mnemonics superimposes an artificial logical structure on data which are not necessarily related.

Mnemonic techniques were possibly first devised by the ancient Greeks.

Mnemonics and oral culture

In oral cultures, the mnemonic system has a different role from the kind of recall that writing permits. It may be used as a repository of collective memory, a system for passing on culture to the next generation, a method for enacting ritual.

Mnemonics can be visual, or a combination of text and pictures.

Visual mnemonics

Visual mnemonics preceded writing and functioned largely as code.
It worked as a kind of map – a visual guide to a territory.

In the sacred technique of the Australian Aborigines known as *tchuringa*,
initiates are provided with a stylized picture of the local territory.

This mnemonic system is not only a guide to the local environment,
symbolically and practically, but also provides information on human
neighbours and the surrounding flora and fauna.

The Incas, a pre-Columbian culture in Peru, used Quipa belts on which
coloured beads were threaded in the form of a code. They were designed
for messengers, who ran from place to place and used the code to
remember their message.

Mnemonic histories

The Ashanti tribe also use visual mnemonics. Their history is largely dynastic. Each king leaves behind a blackened "stool" as an ancestral shrine to which sacrifices can be made. Various objects are associated with the stool, and various marks are made on it.

The drums of the Ashanti also play a role and sometimes have gold death masks attached to them representing great captains and generals that the Ashanti killed in battle.

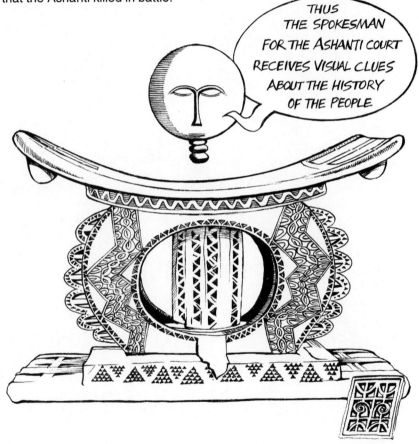

THUS THE SPOKESMAN FOR THE ASHANTI COURT RECEIVES VISUAL CLUES ABOUT THE HISTORY OF THE PEOPLE

The Ojibway of Canada use graphics and drawing to serve a similar purpose. In one form of shamanism, the teacher's version of a myth is promoted by drawings which might map out the journey of a hero or the movement of the clan.

Oral traditions

Most of the world's great religions have strong oral cultures in which
moral laws and sacred texts are memorized in their entirety to preserve
them for posterity.

In Jewish tradition, the word "Mishna" refers to the written record of the
oral law, as opposed to "Mikra", the written law.

Memory as supplement to writing

The memorized law existed alongside the written law. W. Edwards, the editor of the Mishna (now published in written form), wrote in 1911: "It is a point of curious interest to the modern mind that the great mass of knowledge and opinion … was retained in the schools for the most part, perhaps entirely, without the aid of writing. It was transmitted by memory alone, through the process of oral repetition, whence indeed came the title 'Oral Tradition'."

IT IS SIGNIFICANT THAT THE PEOPLE IN CHARGE OF THE PROCESS WERE THE SCRIBES, THE SOPHERIM, WHO WERE THE EXPERTS IN WRITING

The Qur'an

In Islam, the Qur'an exists both as an oral and a written text. As it is rhythmic prose, epic poem and symphony all rolled into one, with every word connected to every other word by rhythm, rhyme and meaning, it is relatively easy to remember.

At any given time, there are literally millions and millions of Muslims who carry the Qur'an, from beginning to end, in their heads.

The Rig Veda

Rig Veda, the sacred text of Hinduism, was transmitted orally from one generation of Brahmins to the next. The Rig Veda contains many mnemonic devices.

The ancient system of learning

The educational system of Western civilization was originally based on seven liberal arts: grammar, rhetoric, dialectic, arithmetic, geometry, music, astronomy.

Rhetoric, the art of speaking and writing with the aim of persuading others, was considered to be of particular importance.

Questions such as: "What is memory?", "Where does it come from?" and "Where is it located in the human body?", acquired significant importance for the ancient world.

Theories of memory

Galen (c. 129–199 AD), the highly influential Graeco-Roman authority on medicine, thought that our memories are kept in our heart and lungs. Many ancient thinkers believed in what we may now call the "white board" theory of memory.

Plato (c. 427–347 BC), the father of philosophy, and his student **Aristotle** (384–322 BC), author of the first book on rhetoric – the greatest thinkers of the ancient world – thought along these lines. But they thought in terms of wax tablets, not "white boards".

Introducing Plato ➤

The Meno

The Meno makes yet another attempt to provide an adequate definition of "virtue". Socrates' final conclusion is that virtue cannot be taught. It is a divine dispensation given to all, even though only a very few are ever able to "recollect" it. Meno then asks Socrates to explain something.

WHAT DO YOU MEAN WHEN YOU SAY THAT WE DON'T LEARN ANYTHING, BUT THAT WHAT WE CALL LEARNING IS RECOLLECTION?

This time, we are probably listening to Plato's ideas rather than those of Socrates. For Plato, knowledge is something we are already born with, and so "learning" is simply forcing this knowledge to resurface into our conscious minds. Socrates neatly illustrates this by asking one of Meno's uneducated slave boys about geometry.

Previous knowledge

Plato believed that knowledge is not derived from sense impressions, but is latent in us. Our souls have knowledge because we *return* to live on earth.

In the *Phaedrus*, Plato argues that the role of rhetoric is to persuade men of the truth – that is, to help them *remember* the truth, a recollection of Ideas seen by all souls of which mere copies exist on earth. Rhetoric, Plato cautioned, should not be used for political agendas, but as an art of speaking the truth.

For Plato, the orator's memory – trained for practical purposes – becomes the philosopher's memory in which he finds "evidence of the divinity and immortality of the soul".

Aristotle

Unlike Plato, Aristotle believed that knowledge is derived from sense impressions. He differentiates between memory and reminiscence or recollection. Recollection is the recovery of knowledge or sensation which one had before. It is a deliberate trawl through the contents of memory, looking for what one is trying to recollect.

In his *De anima*, Aristotle argues that the perceptions brought in by the five senses are first acted upon by the imagination. The images formed by the imagination become the material with which we think.

IMAGINATION IS THE INTERMEDIARY BETWEEN PERCEPTION AND THOUGHT

Memory belonged to the same part of the soul as imagination.

THE IMAGE-MAKING PART OF THE SOUL MAKES THE WORK OF HIGHER PROCESSES OF THOUGHT POSSIBLE

Introducing Aristotle

Imagination and Memory

Imagination is the "movement which results upon an actual sensation". It is the holding up of the image of sensation before the heart (or mind, as we would say), and the retention of the image is, of course, memory.

WE CAN STORE THESE IMAGES AND SORT THROUGH THEM, TO MAKE COMPARISONS WITH NEW SENSATIONS.

AN ILLUSION OR A DREAM IS THE RESULT OF AN ACCIDENTAL RECOLLECTION OF THESE IMAGES.

In a fever, for example, the disruption to the heart from the illness may throw up a disordered and meaningless collection of images.

41

The goddess Memory

The ancient Greek world and its thinkers worshipped memory as a goddess – Mnemosyne, mother of the nine Muses who preside over all of the arts and sciences. Plato, Aristotle and other philosophers who followed long after them, believed strongly in the value of memory training.

The Art of Memory

Between 86 and 82 BC, an unknown teacher in Rome wrote one of the most influential books on rhetoric: *Ad Herennium*. It was extensively used well into the 16th century. The teacher goes through the five parts of rhetoric: *inventio, dispositio, elocutio, memoria, pronuntiatio*. The section on memory starts with the words …

Ad Herennium suggests that memory comes in two segments: "natural" memory which is ingrained in our minds and "artificial" memory which is strengthened by training. But it is a very puzzling training of artificial memory that *Ad Herennium* prescribes, as we'll now see.

The Store house of memory

Artificial memory is established by the literal allocation of places and images. The place or *locus* can be the choice of a house or a path in the forest. The images are forms, marks or simulacra of what we wish to remember.

We can imagine these *loci* as actual "storehouses" in which are kept things we need to recall. This is a complex visual system of pigeon-holing – an architectural memory-bank – very like the rooms of a museum filled with art objects. Orators would "store" long speeches by means of these artificial memory locations.

MEMORY IS MAPPED BY DIFFERENT PLACES THAT I CAN VISIT IN A SWIFT MENTAL JOURNEY...

The orator retrieves all of the words and arguments of his speech by the coded reminder of images attached to them.

The picture palace of memory

We can scarcely imagine how such a bizarre "memory storage" worked.
Marcus Tullius Cicero (106–43 BC) – Roman orator, philosopher and
statesman – casts some light on it in his work on rhetoric, *De Oratore*
(c. 55 BC). He also advises a series of places "clearly set out in order".
But the essence of memorization is in *images* – "active, sharply defined,
unusual" – that penetrate the mind.

The picturing mind

Cicero describes a practice available only to persons with exceptional visual memory. Nevertheless, he offers two significant ideas of memory: first, that we retain most easily in mind what is conveyed by *sight*; second, that memory is a *hiding-place*.

Quintilian's advice on memory

A clearer description of "mnemotechnics" is provided by **Marcus Fabius Quintilian** (c. 35–100 AD), a famous teacher of rhetoric in Rome. Memory often returns upon *revisiting* a place, he sensibly observes, and adds, "as in most cases, art originates from experiment". A spacious house divided into many rooms may be chosen for revisit. What does he say of the images or "signs" placed therein? He advises the use of *metonymy* – a part standing for the whole, for instance …

Quintilian literally shows us round a home – a typically spacious one of the Roman upper class. He begins by placing the first sign "in the forecourt; the second, let us say in the atrium; the remainder are placed in order all around the impluvium …"

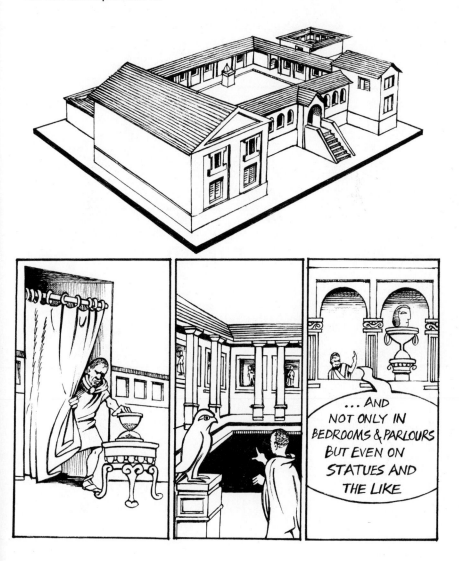

All of these images are linked to one another *as in a chorus* for ease of recall.

Something familiar

Let's pause and consider – is not this "storehouse" of memory familiar to us? Suppose we translate "art of memory" into "technology of memory", what now? Of course, our computer with its icons, menus, chat-rooms, programs, nets, websites, etc., is precisely a "mnemonic system" of retrieval.

Artificial memory or AI?

The ancient belief in artificial memory should also remind us of our own notion of *artificial intelligence* (AI). There is a crucial issue at stake here. AI highlights a very old and perhaps insoluble problem. Is consciousness – or whatever we like to call "mind" – something innate and unique to humans?

Our ideas of artificial intelligence and indeed "virtual reality" have their origin in the ancient quest for the universal laws of communication.

Quintilian the sceptic

Quintilian was a commonsense educator. His monumental *Institutio oratoria* presents rhetorical techniques in an elegant, practical style that will appeal to later Renaissance humanist culture. Quintilian in fact takes a sceptical view of artificial memory.

Quintilian's scepticism is not new to him. Cicero felt the need to defend artificial memory because it had probably been doubted from the start. **Desiderius Erasmus** (1466–1536) was a Dutch Renaissance humanist who advocated Catholic Church reform. He would adopt Quintilian's view and distrust the art of memory as outdated medievalism.

Presence in mind

The most prominent Latin Father of the Church, **St Augustine**
(354–430 AD), was originally a pagan teacher of rhetoric. In his
Confessions, he invokes classical mnemonics as "spacious palaces"
stored up with treasuries of "innumerable images". Augustine ponders
on the enigma of how things not present to the senses can still be
present in memory as images.

As a convert to Christianity, yet always a Platonist, Augustine believes
that the divine is innate in memory. But the God that he seeks in memory
is to be found neither in images nor in places.

Finding God

Artificial memory became a cornerstone of medieval scholastic philosophy; that is, of grand system-building theology best exemplified by the Dominican friar **St Thomas Aquinas** (c. 1225–74). Aquinas relies especially on Aristotle's psychology of mind – knowledge through sense experience and imagination – and not Plato's theory of innate knowledge. Scholasticism also transforms mnemotechnics into a *devotional exercise* …

Neo-Platonist foundations of science

Artificial memory identified with medieval piety would be rejected by enlightened Renaissance humanism. But the question is more complicated. Experimental science which originates in the Renaissance is found compatible with an occult attitude of mind. This seems baffling to us. The answer is that science begins by turning against the Aristotelian foundations of medieval theology – but also turns back to a revived or "neo"-Platonism. Neo-Platonism encourages two apparently contradictory visions of reality …

TRUE KNOWLEDGE IS DISCOVERABLE BECAUSE IT IS **INNATE** TO THE MIND

BUT NEO–PLATONISM ALSO PERMITS A DISCOVERY OF TRUTH THROUGH **MAGIC**

Introducing Quantum Theory shows Galileo taking the experimental route to "acceptable science" …

Classical Physicists

What is the definition of "classical"?

By **classical** is meant those late 19th century physicists nourished on an academic diet of Newton's mechanics and Maxwell's electromagnetism – the two most successful syntheses of physical phenomena in the history of thought.

WITH A SIMPLE INCLINED PLANE AND A METAL SPHERE, I DEMONSTRATED THAT THE GREAT ARISTOTLE'S PHYSICS WAS FLAWED.

OH, STOP SHOWING OFF!

Testing theories by observation had been the hallmark of good physics since **Galileo** (1564–1642). He showed how to devise experiments, make measurements and compare the results with the predictions of mathematical laws.

The interplay of theory and experiment is still the best way to proceed in the world of acceptable science.

Camillo's memory theatre

Galileo is the pioneer of neo-Platonic experimental science. Its occult twin is represented by **Giulio Camillo** (c. 1480–1544) – orator, poet and hermetic philosopher. Camillo designed a wooden memory theatre arranged in seven tiers of complex magical images. Its secret was to be revealed to only one person – Francis I, King of France – who financed it. What is the "secret" of Camillo's theatre?

Camillo's visionary theatre has seven grades of symbolism ranked from the lowest planetary elements to the highest supercelestial level. The world is "memorized" from the heights of a magically activated universe. But who is the spectator in this cosmic memory system? Camillo has reversed the meaning of classical mnemonics …

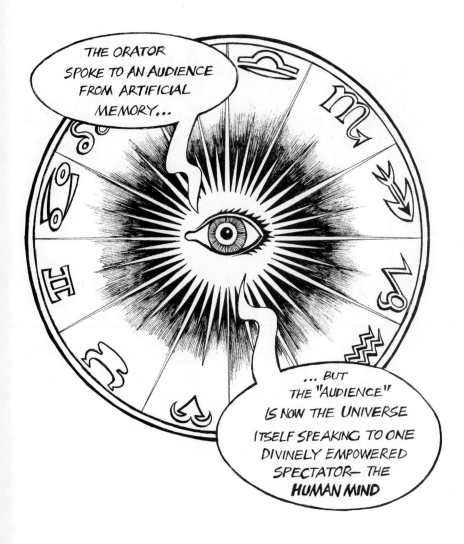

A paradigm shift of mind

Camillo's occult neo-Platonism reflects a paradigm shift in the attitude to learning and remembering. Individual mind is now deemed sufficiently "divine" to embrace universal knowledge. **Giordano Bruno** (1548–1600) – philosopher and Dominican maverick burnt at the stake for heresy – preached the idea that there is "one principle" of the universe innate in memory, which can be retrieved by occult science.

Fludd's memory theatre

"To understand is to speculate with images", Bruno said. "Speculate" is allied to the Latin, *speculum*, "mirror". The mind innately mirrors the true forms of knowledge in Bruno's neo-Platonic art of memory. Bruno's ideas enter an underground current of "black magick" practised by the English Rosicrucian philosopher, **Robert Fludd** (1574–1637). Fludd's occult neo-Platonism is a last-ditch stand against 17th-century experimental science. He also designed a "memory theatre" – at least on paper – of great historical interest to us.

All the world's a stage

Fludd spoke perplexingly of a "round" and a "square" art of memory. The round art places the building in the "heavens" – in the astral zodiac and sphere of planets – and requires the assistance of "daemonic powers". The square art relies on the action of "corporeal images" that may be fictions. Even briefly, we can see how Fludd's system reflects Shakespeare's Globe Theatre with its "celestial round" above a square stage on which fictitious actions take place.

Introducing Shakespeare ➔

ebuilding the Globe Theatre

In the meantime, the American film and theatre impresario **Sam Wanamaker** (1919-93) built a replica of the Globe Theatre, which despite being neither on an original site nor built to exact architectural specifications, begins to occupy the imagination of modern Bardolaters. The International Shakespeare Globe Centre is built on land adjacent to the Rose, but as the Rose was concreted over, work began on the Globe.

Perhaps predictably, Adrian Noble (director of the Royal Shakespeare Company) said: "The answer is not to go back to Globe playhouses. I think that's a nonsense ... because the world has moved on."

The Theory of Everything

Memory began anciently as "Mother of the Muses" but was also to serve as "Mother of Method". It is the pursuit of a *universal method* – a grand unifying *theory* – that explains the confusion of occult and experimental viewpoints on science. **Frances Yates** (1899–1981), in her study *The Art of Memory* (1966), asks what was the "method in the madness" of Camillo, Bruno, Fludd and other system-builders of memory? "[T]here was a fierce scientific impulse in those efforts, a striving after some method of the future, half-glimpsed, half-dreamed of ..."

Introducing Stephen Hawking

It has always profoundly disturbed me that if the laws of physics could break down at the beginning of the Universe, they could also break down anywhere else. That's why we have developed the No Boundary Proposal which removes the singularity at the beginning of the Universe.

But there is a problem with cosmology because it can not predict anything about the Universe without an assumption about the initial conditions. All one can say is that things are as they are *now* because they were as they were at an earlier stage.

Many people believe that this is how it should be and science should be concerned only with laws which govern how the Universe evolves in time. They feel that the initial conditions for the universe that determine how the Universe *began* is a question for metaphysics or religion rather than science.

A scientific reform of memory

Francis Bacon (1561–1626), father of the "inductive method" in experimental science, might reject occult memory but not the utility of the art which he aimed to reform of "superstitious idolatry". His own house at Gorhambury featured mnemonic devices painted on its windows. But the classical discipline of memory had a new scientific purpose for Bacon – to keep "matters in mind" for empirical investigation.

SCIENTIFIC ENQUIRY IS HELPED BY DRAWING AN ORDER OF PARTICULARS FROM A MASS OF NATURAL OBSERVATIONS TO ARRIVE AT INDUCTIVE JUDGEMENTS

The art of memory is turning into a system of *classification* in natural science.

René Descartes (1596–1650), mathematician and philosopher, aimed to eliminate doubt from science by founding its method on the self-evident truths of geometry. He too, like Bacon, outlined a scientific reform of artificial mnemonics. "How do I make myself master of all I discover?", Descartes asks, and replies, "… through the reduction of things to their causes. Since all can be reduced to one, it is obviously not necessary to remember all the sciences."

Descartes' brand of neo-Platonism conceives of the universe as a mathematical code to be solved.

Res Extensa

Descartes held to the Pythagorean and Platonist ideas that the visible world is merely an illusion that hides the mathematical reality of things.

So there is nothing especially new about Descartes' view that we can only ever have knowledge of the mathematically certain *res extensa* (the width, breadth and height of matter that occupies space).

Such knowledge is safe and secure because it lies in the geometric world of clear and distinct propositions.

Properties like hardness and colour are relative, unmeasurable, and are subjective sensations produced in human minds by the objects, but not actually present in them. So objects possess reliable "primary qualities" as well as the odder and more puzzling "secondary qualities".

Introducing Newton and Classical Physics

Newton's vision

Descartes' reduction of reality to "mathematicized certainty" leaves it abstractly grey and lifeless. This was a view uncongenial to the "greatest scientist", **Sir Isaac Newton** (1642–1727), despite the fact that he systematized the mathematical principles of physics. Newton's curiosity led him to strange experiments …

"I push a bodkin betwixt my eye and ye bone as neare to the backside of my eye as I can and pressing my eye with ye end of it there appear several white dark and coloured circles, which circles are plainest when I continue to rub my eye with the point of ye bodkin."

Isaac does not spare himself in researching the phenomenon of colour. Practising what the Neo-Platonists preached, his practical experimentation is carried as far as staring at the Sun until he almost goes blind and sticking blunt needles in behind his eyeball to see the effect.

He finds that Hooke, and indeed everyone else from Aristotle to Descartes, has misunderstood the fundamental nature of light.

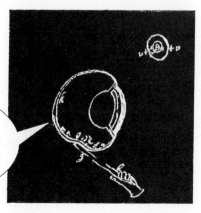

TO RECOVER I SHUT MYSELF UP IN MY CHAMBER MADE DARK FOR THREE DAYS TOGETHER. I BEGAN IN THREE OR FOUR DAYS TO HAVE SOME USE OF MY EYES AGAIN.

Subtle Spirits

His experiments with light have caused him to turn more and more away from Descartes' description of physical reality, the standard mechanical system of nature. He has never been happy with its separation of mind and body, its elimination of the spirit. It conjured up a boring world, free of sound, smell, colour or feeling.

Newton is reported as being, "intent on Chimicall Studies and practices, and beginning to think mathematical speculations to grow at least nice and dry, if not somewhat barren."

Hermetic philosophy because of its experimental nature had a better basis than Descartes' theories. Subtle spirits might just modify Cartesianism in the right direction.

Sir Isaac carried his enquiry very far downwards into the ultimate components of matter, as well as upwards towards the boundless regions of space.

Newton needed to explain the behaviour of the tiniest bodies in order to complete his universal system. Dealing in substances, essences, souls and virtues rather than matter in motion, Isaac, the Alchemist, was searching for no less than the structure of the universe.

A calculus of memory

The great polymath **G.W. Leibniz** (1646–1716) was Newton's rival claimant to the invention of calculus. Leibniz knew well the methods of artificial memory – in particular, the universal system of combining signs, categories and concepts devised by the Franciscan **Ramon Lull** (c. 1235–1315). He recognized how a "calculus" could be adapted from Lull's arrangement of memory images …

The mind works with a logic patterned on the universe.

enfin Leibniz vient

BY REPLACING LULL'S IMAGES WITH **ALGEBRAIC SYMBOLS** IN LOGICAL COMBINATIONS, WE ARRIVE AT INFINITESIMAL CALCULUS

With this step of "mathematicized memory", we pass to the universal language of modern science.

Mechanical man

The picturing itself of memory undergoes empiricist reform as science gains ascendancy in the period of 18th-century Enlightenment. Mind and the human organism in general are reduced to mechanical functions. The prevailing technologies in turn serve as "models" – clocks, the hydraulic pumping machine, and as we enter the 20th century, the telephone exchange system, and finally the computer analogy.

La Mettrie and Helvétius

The most scandalous and extreme materialist of the Enlightenment was a physician, **Julien Offroy de la Mettrie** (1709–51), whose *Homme Machine* (1747) claimed it was possible to explain all human faculties, intellectual and spiritual as well as physical, by the organization of matter, and thus to dispense with the need for any type of soul.

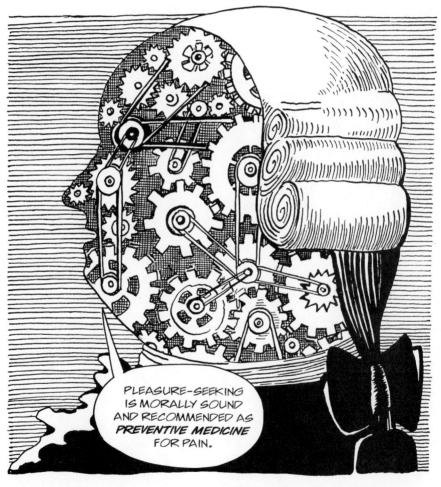

PLEASURE-SEEKING IS MORALLY SOUND AND RECOMMENDED AS *PREVENTIVE MEDICINE* FOR PAIN.

What was most scandalous to his contemporaries – including Diderot and d'Holbach – was la Mettrie's conclusion that there are **no absolute moral standards** and the individual is totally dominated by physical impulses. He was forced to flee, first Paris, then Holland. At the invitation of Frederick the Great, he settled finally in Prussia.

Social mechanisms

Modernity is characterized by the predominant notion of society as itself a *system of unconscious forces* in which we are individually and collectively subsumed. Society becomes an object of science like chemistry or physics. Such was the "positivist" view o**f Auguste Comte** (1798–1857) who coined the term "sociology", further developed by **Emile Durkheim** (1858–1917). Not by chance, Durkheim's key work was on suicide (1897).

Social Facts

Durkheim was very keen to demonstrate the workings of what he called "social facts", which he described as "ways of acting, thinking, and feeling, external to the individual, and endowed with a power of coercion, by reason of which they control him".

This means that certain structures in society are so powerful that they control the actions of individuals and can be studied objectively, as in the natural sciences.

This was positivism at its most extreme.

ARMCHAIR SOCIOLOGIST

Lost memories

Is Durkheim convincing about the "social causes" of suicide? Sociology relies on unconscious collective dynamics to explain individual behaviour. There are no strictly "private" acts. Do we find individuality rescued by Durkheim's contemporary, **Sigmund Freud** (1856–1939), the founder of psychoanalysis? Freud's insight was that "lost" or repressed memories of traumatic events can cause neurotic disabilities.

Freud tried digging into the unconscious by way of hypnotism, "pressure technique" and questioning, until he arrived at free association and dream analysis.

Introducing Freud

THE 'PRESSURE' TECHNIQUE HAS TO GIVE WAY

THE FREE ASSOCIATION TECHNIQUE
Patients must be free, without censorship or urging . . .

Collective memory

The unconscious in Freud's theory is not simply an individual mental state, but has a biological foundation. In this sense, it is collective – a universal structure of the human organism. We can of course "privatize" memory and overlook its debt to collectivity. **Maurice Halbwachs** (1877–1945), another French sociologist, investigated the city of Jerusalem and found its history rewritten by each group of invaders who had conquered, occupied and lost it. Each had to shift the "centre" of Jerusalem to fit in with their own history …

Halbwachs considered it essential to listen attentively to these different voices so that tolerance, understanding and peace might at last prevail in the Middle East.

Halbwachs perished in the Nazi concentration camp at Buchenwald.

The haunted past

Collective memory plays a crucial role in the foundation of social identity. The past is not only commemorated but institutionalized in museums, in books, on film and television. Such representation is often deeply problematic. The past is full of painful memories that we have not yet come to terms with.

Post-Colonial Discourse

Orientalism spawned a whole genre of critical writings known variously as post-colonial studies, post-colonial theory and post-colonial discourse. The term "post-colonial" does not imply "after colonialism".

Behaviourist theory of learning

Behaviourism is an extreme mechanistic psychology formulated by **Ivan Pavlov** (1849–1936), **J.B. Watson** (1878–1958) and **B.F. Skinner** (1904–90). It reduces all learning to a "conditioned reflex", i.e., the response of an organism to specific stimuli.

Pavlov famously conditioned a dog to salivate whenever it heard the sound of a bell – even if no food was present.

The Skinner Box

Behaviourism presupposes that mind is simply an imprintable "blank surface" – just like the "wax tablet" theory of artificial memory. This is an idea originally found in Aristotle and later refined by the British empiricist philosopher **John Locke** (1632–1704).

A crude reduction of mind

Behavioural experiments tell us something about *control* and *predictability*, but not how the mind makes unpredictably new discoveries. Behaviourism wished to eliminate consciousness altogether from the scientific agenda. But the problem revived in the 1960s with further investigations of the brain, advances in artificial intelligence and cognitive science.

THE COMPUTER SEEMS TO PROVIDE AN EXPLANATORY MODEL OF INTELLIGENCE...

...WE CAN THINK OF THE MIND AS "SOFTWARE" AND THE BRAIN AS "HARDWARE"

Introducing Consciousness

The Turing Test

The British mathematician and inventor of the modern computer, **Alan Turing** (1912–54), believed that intelligent computers would be built fairly soon. In support of this conjecture, he devised the "Turing Test" as a criterion for computer consciousness.

Imagine you are communicating with some being via some remote device, like a telex or e-mail. You can't tell directly if you are talking to a machine or a person, because you can't see it. But you can ask it questions, discuss its responses, and so on.

And anything that can pass this test, argued Alan Turing, ought to be credited with the same kind of consciousness as we have.

Is it all in the brain?

Turing's test does not resolve the difference between *simulating* a conscious mind and really having one. The problem of *self*-consciousness remains baffling. Is the answer already there in the complex workings of the human brain?

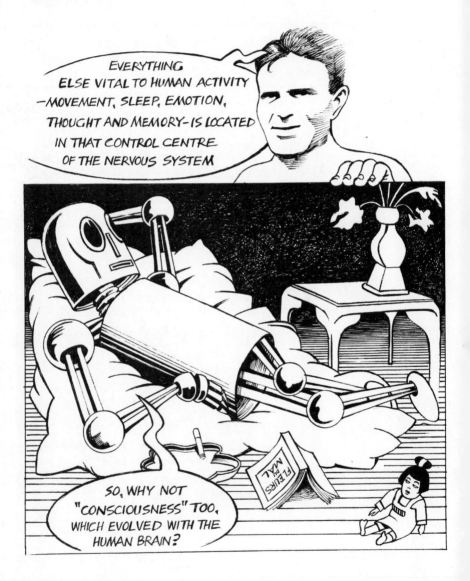

EVERYTHING ELSE VITAL TO HUMAN ACTIVITY —MOVEMENT, SLEEP, EMOTION, THOUGHT AND MEMORY—IS LOCATED IN THAT CONTROL CENTRE OF THE NERVOUS SYSTEM

SO, WHY NOT "CONSCIOUSNESS" TOO, WHICH EVOLVED WITH THE HUMAN BRAIN?

How does the brain work?

There are two types of brain cells: *neurons*, which number 100,000,000,000; and even more numerous *neuroglia* of which little is known. Neurons vary, but all have a cell body (*axon*) and branching fibres (*dendrites*).

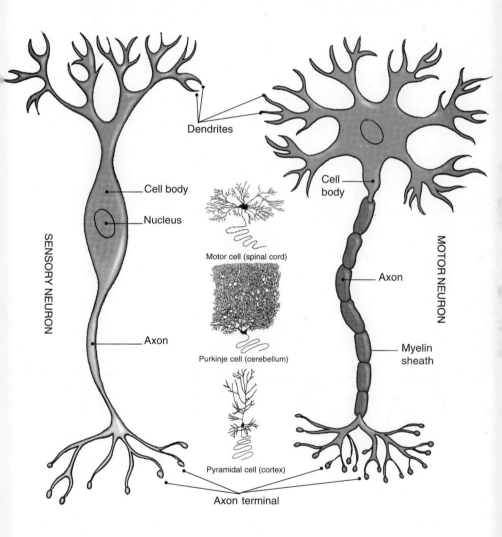

SENSORY NEURON

MOTOR NEURON

Dendrites

Cell body

Nucleus

Cell body

Axon

Axon

Myelin sheath

Motor cell (spinal cord)

Purkinje cell (cerebellum)

Pyramidal cell (cortex)

Axon terminal

The brain functions by the "irritability" of neurons, which responds to both electrical and chemical signals. Let's look at the axon's release of chemical transmitters …

The Chemical Brain

Where axon branches connect to the dendrites or bodies of target cells there is a small gap, which **Sir Charles Scott Sherrington** (1857-1952) named the **synapse**. The electrical potential coming down the axon cannot jump this gap. Instead, the **pre-synaptic** axon releases specially shaped chemical **molecules**.

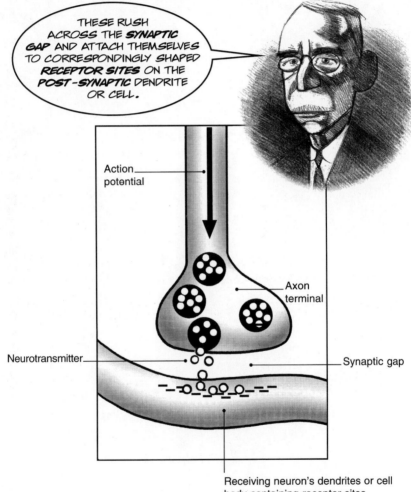

THESE RUSH ACROSS THE *SYNAPTIC GAP* AND ATTACH THEMSELVES TO CORRESPONDINGLY SHAPED *RECEPTOR SITES* ON THE *POST-SYNAPTIC* DENDRITE OR CELL.

Action potential

Axon terminal

Neurotransmitter

Synaptic gap

Receiving neuron's dendrites or cell body containing receptor sites

If the next cell is another neuron, arrival of the molecules will either increase (excitatory) or decrease (inhibitory) the likelihood of that cell firing.

These specially shaped chemical molecules – neurotransmitters – are decisive for proper brain functioning.

A complex network

Let's reconsider some of these chemical neurotransmitters. Acetylcholine is found not only in the brain but in muscle cells and nerves. It plays a role in sleep, wakefulness and arousal. Dopamine is involved in movement. Noradrenaline transmitter, derived from dopamine, increases alertness.

In other words, brain and body are not separate, but co-ordinated in networks of organic activity that provide for what we call "mind".

Brain, Hormones and Body

Neurotransmitters are similar in many respects to **hormones**. Hormones, such as **adrenaline** and **testosterone**, are secreted into the blood by glands. In the blood, they can travel to affect distant organs.

Hormones regulate bodily functions, such as energy production and metabolism.

AND THEY ARE INVOLVED IN CONTROL OF EMOTIONAL, SEXUAL AND OTHER BEHAVIOURS.

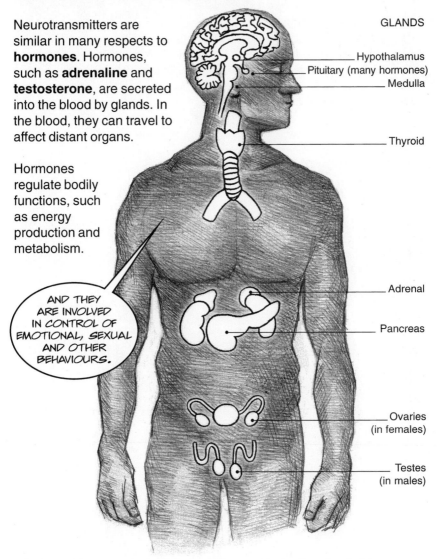

GLANDS

Hypothalamus
Pituitary (many hormones)
Medulla

Thyroid

Adrenal

Pancreas

Ovaries
(in females)

Testes
(in males)

• Brain activity controls the release of hormones by the glands into the blood.
• But hormones, carried up to the brain in the blood, then serve to influence the activity of the brain itself.
• The brain is a bodily organ, part of a larger functioning system. When, as in this book, we focus exclusively on the brain, we easily lose sight of this fact.

91

How does the brain learn?

Let's consider the humble sea slug, Aplysia, with only 5,000 neurons. If its head is touched, it responds with a defensive withdrawal of its gill. But when touched repeatedly, the gill withdrawal response ceases, i.e., it "habituates" or learns to *ignore a stimulus*. But, after habituation, a mild shock to Aplysia's body will produce an increased withdrawal response, i.e., it shows *sensitization*.

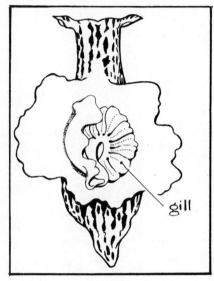

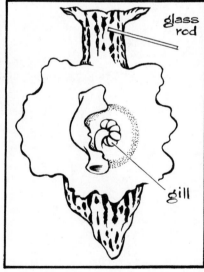

The slug responds by a change in the levels of its neurotransmitters – but its "memory" lasts only an hour or so. We retain memories far longer.

Learning by experience

Studies on Marsh Tits show that the hippocampus region of the brain increases in size as young birds develop the ability to remember things. Marsh Tits store food in hiding places and then retrieve it later – an example of memory. One group of young birds was allowed to store and retrieve food as usual, while another group was not: they were fed with seed that could not be carried away.

Brain damage

A patient suffered injury to the thalamus part of the brain. After an initial period of amnesia, he could remember everything up to two weeks before the accident. His learning skills were also affected.

Conclusion: we can assume that the temporal lobe and the thalamus must play different roles in memory.

Left and right brain theory

Humans are unique in being left- or right-handed – rarely both. Other primates may also be right- or left-handed, but we are the only species with a "consistent bias to the same side". It would seem natural to think that the two hemispheres of the brain must also show some consistent bias. For several decades, it was assumed that the left cerebral hemisphere is the logical, verbal and dominant half of the brain, while the right is the imaginative, emotional, spatially aware but suppressed side. Thus, two personalities exist in one head.

The evidence of split brains

The myth grew largely from the "split brain" research carried out during the 1960s.

Nobel Laureate **Roger Sperry** (1913–94), of the California Institute of Technology, carried out drastic surgery on epileptic patients. He cut the corpus callosum – the thick bundle of nerve fibres that forms the main connection between the cerebral hemispheres. These split-brain patients were then given tests in matching objects. The left hemisphere (LH) should match by *function*, the right (RH) by *appearance*.

SO, WHEN PRESENTED WITH A CAKE ON A PLATE, THE **LH** OUGHT TO CONNECT TO A PICTURE OF A FORK OR SPOON...

...THE **RH** SHOULD SELECT A PICTURE OF A BROAD-BRIMMED HAT

One very curious finding is that after the operation previously right-handed people draw better with their **left** hands. (Performance with either hand is worse than pre-operatively.) This comes about because the left hand is controlled by the RH and the right hand by the LH. In intact brains, the two hemispheres share their abilities and knowledge via the corpus callosum, so both would contribute to the movements of a right hand.

Left-hand drawing   Models   Right-hand drawing

AFTER SPLIT-BRAIN SURGERY, HOWEVER, THE SPATIAL ABILITIES OF THE RH ARE AVAILABLE ONLY TO THE LESS SKILFUL LEFT HAND.

A clear-cut case?

Sperry concluded that surgery revealed "two spheres of consciousness" locked in one head: the LH with speech and rationality; the RH inarticulate but blessed with special spatial abilities.

But are the left and right hemispheres so clear cut in functions? Doubts began to appear when researchers discovered that damage to part of the right hemisphere destroys the natural melody of speech.

Human consciousness has been probed by behavioural experiment, studies in brain damage and electro-encephalography (EEG). New computer-linked techniques are available: Positron Emission Topography (PET) and Magnetic Resonance Imaging (MRI). These give us amazing pictures of which brain areas are activated by which mental tasks.

Perhaps we must look not only at the brain but at the whole *genetic structure* of humans? Here we run against the problem of *differences* between people that are not exclusively dictated by genes.

Introducing Evolution ▶

Genes and Environment

Take any two humans and compare them. They will resemble each other in many ways, because they have many genes in common, but they will not be perfectly identical.

Some of the differences between them will be due to the fact that they have different genes.

*Other differences will be due to the fact that they have grown up in **different environments**.*

*Development is not determined by genes alone, but by a **combination** of genetic and environmental factors.*

Despite the name, "identical" twins are never perfectly alike. The differences between identical twins cannot be due to genetic differences, since they have the same genes. All the differences between identical twins must therefore be due to differences in their environments.

Genetics might seem to offer the "final explanation" of all behaviour. We expect miracles from it – the elimination of mortal diseases, the remedy to crime, and – for some – the way to increase intelligence!

Introducing Genetics

Get those genes into him; he'll be famous in the end!

The holistic brain

It is now clear that the activity of the entire brain system is incredibly complicated. We no longer accept that certain "pigeon-holed" areas of the brain are "responsible" for particular thoughts and memories – these are dispersed among connective webs. A new memory appears to affect every single neuron in our brain, not just one side or part. Such messages are not imprinted in any permanent place, but become part of a changing and adaptable memory system. And this system has enormous capacity – about 200 billion neurons …

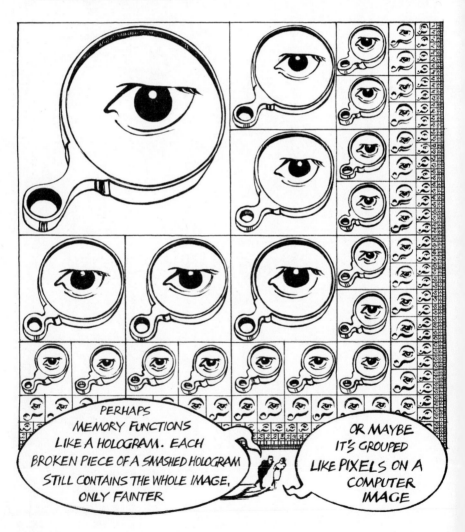

The child's astonishing brain

We come into the world with 100 billion neurons in place and ten times as many support cells. Each child's experiences are unique – from within the womb and throughout the years of maturation. Our brains grow at an astonishing rate – doubling in size during the first two years and increasing by 400 per cent by sixteen years of age.

The plasticity of learning

Connections in the brain strengthen and grow as they are used. Fingers and the mouth have a greater allocation of neurons than the back, because they are used more and are highly agile. The brain cells that are used most frequently will have extensive connections, whereas those that are not used so much are pushed aside. This is called "neuronal plasticity".

Young children have the most fertile imaginations and voracious appetites for learning. They learn by making associations between objects. This need for learning raises the great question of **teaching** …

Beat it into them!

Teaching is in essence that by which a child *learns to learn*. Is there a "best method" of teaching? Traditional theories of learning have been generally "behaviourist", i.e., based on a stimulus-response framework that aims to change behaviour. Western civilization has tended to deal with knowledge as a commodity to be transmitted, more or less intact, from teacher to student.

Occult memory in education

The Czech religious leader **Jan Amos Comenius** (1592–1670) was an enlightened educator. He had the revolutionary idea that teachers ought to "follow in the footsteps of nature" by considering *how* children learn. He invented a picture-book primer for children, the *Orbis pictus* (1658). By looking at a picture of the sun, a child learned the word for it in different languages – a totally original idea now become commonplace. How did the idea of learning by pictures occur to Comenius?

Introducing Rousseau ▶

Progressive Educationalists

Rousseau's doctrine of the "natural innocence" of children is allied to his conception of "Natural men" who are free of all civilized evils. Children therefore require a special kind of education. Freedom and happiness in childhood are crucial because whatever is experienced then will determine adult behaviour. This means that negative behaviour is always *acquired* – the adult bully must inevitably have been bullied as a child. This idea of "childhood creativity" influenced many 19th-century Romantics, especially those who spearheaded "progressive education", like the Swiss social reformer **J.H. Pestalozzi** (1746-1827) and later **Maria Montessori** (1870-1952).

The problem is that Rousseau's "system" remains immune from any possibility of children's bad behaviour.

Three main theories

Contemporary theories of learning come in three varieties: *behavioural*, *cognitive* and *social*. Behavioural theories see the learner as reactive. Cognitive theories stress the role of mental processes in the acquisition of knowledge. Social theories are concerned with individual participation in a community of learners.

Most current theories accept that meaningful learning is an active, self-regulated, constructive, cumulative and goal-oriented process.

Learning mechanisms

The American cognitive theorist, T.J. Shuell of State University of New York, has identified twelve "learning functions" necessary for meaningful learning to take place.

1. Establishing expectations
2. Establishing motivation
3. Activating prior knowledge
4. Focusing attention on relevant features of the material being studied
5. Encoding information
6. Comparing information
7. Generating hypotheses about possible relationships and solutions
8. Repetition of information until it is integrated into higher-level concepts
9. Receiving feedback on adequacy of one's understanding
10. Evaluating one's hypotheses and the feedback received
11. Monitoring the learning/understanding process
12. Combining, integrating and synthesizing available information to form a new (revised) understanding of the topic being studied

Equally as an individual mental process or as a social process, learning involves making connections, exploring patterns and grasping the "bigger picture" in its details. And nothing helps you better in establishing connections than *pictures*.

A picture test

In a famous experiment published in *Scientific American* (1970), memory researcher Ralph Haber tested people's ability to remember pictures. Volunteers were shown 2,500 slides, one image shown every ten seconds. After a break of one hour, the volunteers were shown 2,500 pairs of slides.

A high memory score

The accuracy rate was astonishing – between 80 and 95 per cent. Haber concluded: "These experiments suggest that the recognition of pictures is essentially perfect. The results would probably have been the same if we had used 25,000 pictures."

But not any old pictures will do. Not every picture helps you to learn. Just as it is easier to remember a meaningful sequence than a random set of events, the pictures accompanying a text have to be meaningfully co-ordinated. The brain loves pattern: so, if a pattern can be woven between words and images, the connections become memorable.

In *Introducing* books, text and illustrations are married, so the whole is much greater than the sum of the parts. The books use the whole brain in allowing the reader to take in sequential, textual information as well as the holistic, visual information.

A new "art of memory"

Illustrators faced with often abstract subjects respond by drawing on wide-ranging references to visual culture. Here are two examples from *Introducing Mathematics* …

The illustrator's aim is to trigger imaginative *associations* and connections that will engage the reader and imprint the information on the long-term memory web. On another page, one of the *Mathematics* authors, Zia Sardar, discusses the metric system introduced during the French Revolution …

Now our measurements are based on science.

The "Système Internationale" is descended from the "metric system" that was introduced during the French Revolution. It provides a connected set of units derived from basic quantities, such as the metre (m) for length, the second (s) for time, and the kilogram (kg) for mass. Most of the practical measures are expressed in powers of ten of the units, such as millimetre (mm) for length.

Time is an exception – the attempt by the French reformers to divide the month into three "decades" of ten days, and then the day into ten hours of a hundred minutes each, was very unpopular, and so we still use the system invented in Babylon.

Zia Sardar: author

Just as Cicero advised the orators of ancient times to create "memorable images", so too the illustrations of the *Introducing* series are designed to evoke strong memories. Another example from *Introducing Stephen Hawking* shows Einstein's "thought experiment" that led him to his theory of relativity: "For an observer falling freely, there exists no gravitational field."

Pagan Virtù and Christian Virtue

Machiavelli's general advice is to be bold rather than timid. In the words of the maxim, "Fortune favours the brave."

...BEING A WOMAN, SHE FAVOURS YOUNG MEN, BECAUSE THEY ARE LESS CIRCUMSPECT AND MORE ARDENT, AND BECAUSE THEY COMMAND HER WITH GREATER AUDACITY.

THE WORD DOES NOT DESCRIBE A "GOOD" OR "VIRTUOUS" PERSON IN THE USUAL SENSE.

This ability – call it vigour, prowess, bravery, pride, courage, strength – was what Machiavelli called **virtù** (from the Latin *virtus*, itself from *vir*, man). In other words, **virtù** describes the qualities desirable for a man which include a certain ruthlessness.

Machiavelli's idea of *virtù* – opposed to the Christian notion of "virtue" – prescribes a ruthless quality to be as necessary to a ruler's success as good Fortune. The illustration dramatizes *virtù* by reference to a duet of film icons – Marlon Brando, in *On the Waterfront* (1954), embracing the uncertainty of "Fortune" portrayed as a faceless female, with Orson Welles, the charismatic rogue in *The Third Man* (1949), looking out of the shadows.

The length of memory

A cross-fertilization of words and images will help the memory to retain material – but for how long? Research has found that a maximum retention period can stretch to many years with fairly stable access to the information. Of course, accessibility will depend on how much we rehearse our memories. This was tested in a scientific study by German psychologist **Hermann Ebbinghaus** (1850–1909).

How long might anyone be expected to retain such non-referential material?

If he repeated the syllables 64 times on the first day, he took only seven minutes to relearn them on the following day. If he repeated them only eight times on day one, he took nearly 20 minutes to relearn them on day two. How long did it take for these syllables to become permanent memories?

Ebbinghaus' methodology has now become a standard procedure in human learning laboratories.

Keep taking the tablets

So, if you want to remember things better, start by reviewing them early. Read your *Introducing* book at the very beginning of the course – say, for instance, *Introducing Machiavelli*, if you're taking a course in political history. Re-read it during the course. Each reading will bring out the richness of the illustrated text-tapestry. You will discover new connections – see illustrations in new ways – and get visual jokes that you missed last time.

Towards postmodernism

You will have noticed how in this book we explored a number of different disciplines, while focusing on the specific subjects of learning and memory. We journeyed from the ancient art of memory to computers, touched on Renaissance occultism and the origins of science, delved into neuro-science on our way through art, philosophy, history and educational theories.

Only connect ...

No subject exists in isolation. This has been postmodernism's most fruitful lesson. Knowledge does not remain neatly compartmentalized into disciplines, but spills over and "transgresses" boundaries.

A Hebrew proverb says: "Do not confine your children to your own learning, for they were born in a different time."

One vast library

The Name of the Rose (1984), a mystery novel by the semiotician **Umberto Eco** (b. 1932), conceives of the world as one vast library – with books everywhere, past and present, all talking to other books – an idea borrowed from the Argentinian writer and blind librarian **Jorge Luis Borges** (1899–1986). How does one enter into this universal discourse? One way is to begin with *Introducing*'s illustrated series …

Extracts in this book have been taken from the following *Introducing* titles:

Page 5	*Introducing Einstein* (1999), image from p. 92
Page 6	*Introducing Wittgenstein* (1999), p. 116
Page 10	*Introducing Critical Theory* (2001), p. 72
Page 37	*Introducing Plato* (2000), p. 44
Page 41	*Introducing Aristotle* (2001), p. 114
Page 57	*Introducing Quantum Theory* (1999), p. 5
Page 63	*Introducing Shakespeare* (2001), p. 118
Pages 65, 116	*Introducing Stephen Hawking* (1999), pp. 156, 34
Page 68	*Introducing Descartes* (1999), p. 98
Pages 69, 70	*Introducing Newton and Classical Physics* (2000), pp. 91, 105
Page 73	*Introducing the Enlightenment* (1999), p. 88
Page 75	*Introducing Sociology* (1999), p. 42
Page 77	*Introducing Freud* (1999), images from pp. 40, 41
Page 81	*Introducing Cultural Studies* (1999), p. 115
Page 85	*Introducing Consciousness* (1999), p. 90
Pages 87, 88, 91, 97	*Introducing Mind and Brain* (1999), pp. 31, 35, 37, 117
Page 100	*Introducing Evolution* (2001), p. 54
Page 101	*Introducing Genetics* (2000), p. 155
Page 107	*Introducing Rousseau* (2001), p. 73
Pages 114, 115	*Introducing Mathematics* (1999), pp. 61, 49
Pages 117, 118	*Introducing Machiavelli* (1999), pp. 119, 70

Other titles in the *Introducing* series:

Introducing American Politics
Introducing Barthes
Introducing Baudrillard
Introducing Walter Benjamin
Introducing Buddha
Introducing Camus
Introducing Chaos
Introducing Chomsky
Introducing Christianity
Introducing Darwin and Evolution
Introducing Derrida
Introducing Eastern Philosophy
Introducing Environmental Politics
Introducing Ethics
Introducing Evolutionary Psychology
Introducing Existentialism
Introducing Fascism and Nazism
Introducing Feminism
Introducing Foucault
Introducing Fractal Geometry
Introducing Hegel

Introducing Heidegger
Introducing the Holocaust
Introducing Islam
Introducing Joyce
Introducing Jung
Introducing Kafka
Introducing Kant
Introducing Keynesian Economics
Introducing Lacan
Introducing Lenin and the Russian Revolution
Introducing Lévi-Strauss and Structural Anthropology
Introducing Linguistics
Introducing Marquis de Sade
Introducing Marx
Introducing Media Studies
Introducing Melanie Klein
Introducing Modernism
Introducing Nietzsche
Introducing Philosophy

Introducing Postfeminism
Introducing Postmodernism
Introducing Psychoanalysis
Introducing Psychology
Introducing Romanticism

Introducing Sartre
Introducing Semiotics
Introducing Time
Introducing Trotsky and Marxism
Introducing the Universe

In case of difficulty in purchasing any Icon title through normal channels, books can be purchased through BOOKPOST. Tel: + 44 (0)1624 836000 Fax: + 44 (0)1624 837033. E-mail: bookshop@enterprise.net. www.bookpost.co.uk Please quote "Ref: Faber" when placing your order.
If you require further assistance, please contact: info@iconbooks.co.uk

Further reading

The best source on rapidly changing theories of learning is the brand new and truly massive *International Encyclopaedia of the Social and Behavioural Sciences,* edited by N. J. Smelser and P. B. Baltes (Oxford: Pergamon, 2001). The on-line version is constantly updated.

Memory, edited by Patricia Fara and Karalyn Patterson (Cambridge: Cambridge University Press, 1998), is a truly brilliant collection of essays exploring the subject from a number of different perspectives.

Susan Greenfield's *Brain Story* and *The Private Life of the Brain* (both London: Penguin, 2000) are well written and right up to date.

R. L. Gregory, *Eye and Brain* (London: Weidenfeld and Nicolson, 1966) is so good that it has gone through four revised editions (the latest: Fourth Estate, 1990).

Frances A. Yates' *The Art of Memory* (London: Routledge and Kegan Paul, 1966) is an enthralling, not to say classic, exploration of artificial memory techniques from ancient times to the Renaissance.

E.H. Gombrich's *Art and Illusion* (London: Phaidon Press, 1960) has acquired a well-deserved reputation.

Biographies

Ziauddin Sardar has written *Islam, Cultural Studies, Chaos, Media Studies* and *Science,* and co-authored *Postmodernism* and *Mathematics* in this series. The most recent of his thirty or so other books include *Postmodernism and the Other, Orientalism* and *The Consumption of Kuala Lumpur.* A regular contributor to *New Statesman,* his collection of essays, *The A to Z of Postmodern Life,* will be published in early 2002.

Richard Appignanesi is editorial director of Icon Books. He is also the author of *Introducing Freud, Introducing Existentialism* and *Introducing Postmodernism,* and of the forthcoming *Yukio Mishima: Terror and Postmodern Japan* (2002).

Ralph Edney trained as a mathematician, and has worked as a teacher, journalist and political cartoonist. He is the author of two graphic novels, and the illustrator of *Introducing Fractal Geometry* and *Introducing Time.* He is also a cricket fanatic.

Index